ISBN 978-1-332-23271-0
PIBN 10301944

FB &c Ltd, Dalton House, 60 Windsor Avenue, London, SW19 2RR.
Company number 08720141. Registered in England and Wales.

OVER SANDS TO THE LAKES;

BY

EDWIN WAUGH,

AUTHOR OF "SKETCHES OF LANCASHIRE LIFE AND LOCALITIES" "COME WHOAM TO THI CHILDER AN' ME," ETC., ETC.

A. IRELAND & CO., 22, MARKET STREET, MANCHESTER;

AND ALL BOOKSELLERS AND NEWS VENDORS.

—

1860.

OVER SANDS TO THE LAKES.

From Silverdale to Kent sand side,
Whose soil is sown with cockle shells;
From Cartmel eke, and Connyside,
With fellows fierce from Furness fells.

Lancashire Ballad of Flodden Field.

Morecambe Bay, or, the great crooked bay, which divides the districts of Furness and Cartmel from the rest of Lancashire, and which receives the waters of the Wyre, the Lune, the Keer, the Winster, the Kent, the Leven, and other rivers of less note, is a grand object, lying among scenes of singular interest and beauty. Its picturesquely-irregular shores are full of varied charms—soft secluded vales, and green nooks of nestling—old towns and villages, rich parks, and wildwoods sloping to the water—which are all the more charming that they cling like a garland about this play-ground of the capricious sea, with the outlines of the mountains crowding round in the rearward, tier over tier, in stormy majesty. Within the fine sweep of scenery overlooking this bay, there is many a venerable home of ancient religion, many a towered steep and storied glen, that wakes the memories of a thousand years gone by. Morecambe is, also, the outfall of Windermere and Coniston waters, and is the most impressive gateway to the Lake Country. From its shores at Ulverstone, the river Leven will lead the traveller by windings full of changeful beauty, nine miles, to that pleasant resting-place called "Newby Bridge," at the foot of Windermere. Cartmel and Furness have been comparatively unknown, on account of difficulty of access in days gone by; but now that the line from Lancaster to Ulverstone skirts these sequestered regions, their attractions cannot fail to arrest the attention of all lovers of the picturesque in nature. In addition to its natural beauty, Furness is indeed "a land whose stones are iron, and out of whose hills thou mayest dig brass;" but the wild fells and green valleys of Cartmel know little of the bustling world, save what belongs to their purely agricultural and pastoral character; and the primitive race of mountain folk dwelling therein clings to the manners, language, and traditions of its "fore-elders" with an affection little disturbed by communion with the great changes of modern life. To the scholar and student of manners, to the lover of nature, and the man of science, these secluded hills and glens teem with rich and rare interest.

Before the railway was made, the old way of crossing the sands from Lancaster to Ulverstone must have been very striking, both from the character of the scenery around and a sense of danger, which cannot but have given something of the piquancy of adventure to the journey. The channels are constantly shifting, particularly after heavy rains, when they are perilously uncertain. For many centuries past, two guides have conducted travellers over them. Their duty is to observe the changes, and find fordable points. In all seasons and states of the weather this was their duty, and in times of storm and fog it must have been fraught with danger. These guides were anciently appointed by the Prior of Cartmel, and received synodal and Peter-pence for their maintenance. They are now paid from the revenues of the duchy. The office of guide has been so long held by a family of the name of Carter, that the country people have given that name to the office itself. A gentleman, crossing from Lancaster, once

"OVER SANDS."

asked the guide if "Carters" were never lost on the sands. "I never knew any lost," said the guide; "there's one or two drowned now and then, but they're generally found somewhere i'th bed when th' tide goes out." A certain ancient mariner, called Nuttall, who lives at Grange, on the Cartmel shore, told me that "people who get their living by 'following the sands,' hardly ever die in their beds. They end their days on the sands;

and even their horses and carts are generally lost there. I have helped," said he, "to pull horses and coaches, ay, and guides too, out of the sands. The channel," he continued, "is seldom two days together in one place. You may make a chart one day, and, before the ink is dry, it will have shifted." I found, indeed, by inquiry, that those who have travelled the sands longest, are always most afraid of them; and that these silent currents, which shimmer so beautifully in the sunshine, have been "the ribs of death" to thousands. The old "Over Sands" route began at Hest Bank, a cliff on the shore, about three miles from Lancaster. The coach, and whatever travellers might be going, used to meet the guide on the banks of the river Keer, which runs over the sands, about three miles from Hest Bank. Here the guide carefully tried the bed of the stream before travellers were allowed to cross,—for what was fordable yesterday to-day might be a quicksand. The safe tracks are indicated by branches of furze, called "brogs," stuck in the sand. The old word "brog," means a broken branch; and it is very likely that the word "brob," applied by the people of Furness and Cartmel to these furze branches, is merely a corruption of the former word. On reaching Kent's Bank, the coach went about three miles through the villages on the Cartmel shore, and then forward across the Leven estuary, to Ulverstone town. These sands, though not one-third the distance of the sands between Lancaster and Kent's Bank, are considered much more dangerous. Probably the difference may arise from the greater number of persons crossing from Cartmel to Ulverstone. In every village, and in almost every house I entered, upon the shores of this bay, I met with tales of danger and disaster which have occurred upon these sands; and, even now, there is a kind of daily excitement there, arising from the dangerous possibilities of travelling over them. Such was the old "Over Sands" route from Lancaster. In Mrs. Hemans' letters, she thus alludes to the journey:—"I must not omit to tell you that Mr. Wordsworth not only admired our exploit in crossing the Ulverstone sands as a deed of 'derring do,' but as a decided proof of taste. The lake scenery, he says, is never seen to such advantage as after the passage of what he calls its majestic barrier."

This impressive scene may now be traversed by all who prefer speed and ease to danger and delay, free from the uncertainties of the old route. Along the picturesque northern shores of this "majestic barrier," the new line of railway from Lancaster to Ulverstone winds by Silverdale, with the grand features of land and sea full in sight; and the traveller lakewards may, at comparatively little cost of time and money, look upon a scene so strikingly different to what he will find in the country he is going to, that the variety itself cannot but add to the interest of his journey. The length of the line from Carnforth, six miles beyond Lancaster, to Ulverstone is about twenty miles, and, though it passes through one or two rural villages which hide the sea for a few minutes, two-thirds of its length commands a continually changing view of Morecambe Bay. It often runs over large tracts of the sands, where the waves sometimes come lashing the firm embankment, like ocean skirmishers sent out from the main body to remonstrate with this bold invader of their old domain. On the landward side, every mile brings a new picture; the land is full of changeful picturesqueness of indentation, and the shelving shores of light-hued limestone rock, which we pass now and then, are rich in exquisite variety of form and colour. The woods are peculiarly beautiful to look upon, their lighter shades of green being charmingly relieved by numbers of the dark historic yew tree, full of brave remembrances of England and its forest life in the olden time. Here, where the rugged selvedge of our mountain district softens into slopes of fertile beauty by the fitful sea,—and where the mountain streams, at last, wind silently homewards over the sands, we flit by many a sylvan nook, and many a country nest, where we should be glad to linger;—and by the outlet of many a little paradisal glen, nestling in the verdant creases of Cartmel's fells, which, once seen, will nevermore be willingly forgotten, but remain a bower of beautiful remembrance, where the mind may find a resting-place even in the city's busy throng.

Early in the month of May I found myself, one fine evening, walking about the platform of Carnforth Station, waiting for the train to Ulverstone. It was that delightful time of day when the birds were beginning to get stiller, and might be heard more distinctly than before, singing their little nestward solos with drowsy delight, here and there among the trees. The train started, and for the first time I was rolling towards Ulverstone, by way of the Cartmel shore. We were soon over the little river Keer, which, having left the hills, comes gliding through a green plain on the right, and then on across the Lancaster sands, where its shifty channel has been the death-bed of many a gallant man. Now we came to Silverdale Station, where brown-faced, stalwart men were unloading timber, or lounging about the wholesome looking, work-a-day village. In a few minutes we are off again. Gardens, and comfortable stone-built farm-houses, and little orchards all white with apple-blossom are flitting past, and the ragged summits of Cartmel Fells draw nearer to the eye.

Just before reaching the temporary station at Arnside we catch a glimpse of Arnside Tower, a massive old peel, on an eminence at the head of a solitary vale to seaward. In the northward distance there is a fine view of the Cumberland hills at this point. Delightful Arnside! If any man loves the beautiful in nature—if he be a geologist, or a botanist, or an invalid in search of peaceful restoration—let him wander about Arnside, and pleasant Silverdale—which is close by. Shortly after this evening ride I returned for a ramble about Arnside, one sunny day, in company with Mr. W. Salmon, president of the Horticultural Society of Ulverstone, and Mr. Bolton, of Swartmoor, a notable geologist, and a personal "friend and fellow-labourer" of Professor Sedgwick. The day was so fine, and the scene so beautiful, that we were as blithe as three lads going a-nutting to the woods on a holiday morning in summer time. The old station-master at Arnside knew the names of the hills around, and every remarkable point of the glorious landscape. We chatted with him a few minutes, watching the beautiful effect of a cloud-shadow gliding over the grand limestone crags of "Whitbarrow" in the sunlight; and, after begging a few matches, we lit our cigars, and took up a shady lane towards the picturesque hill called "Arnside Knot." Having wound up this pleasant lane, between tall bushy hedgerows, about half a mile, we met the gamekeeper, who gave us directions for the ascent of the "Knot," warning us carefully against the use of fire, by which considerable damage had been done in the woods above. Skirting the eastern slope of the hill, a good road brought us into the vale at the head of which "Arnside Tower," a massive old quadrangular building, of limestone, stands, a lonesome, gloomy-looking ruin. It is finely situated on an isthmus which connects the two peninsulas of Arnside and Silverdale. Seaward, it commands a view of Warton Sands, and looks right over the bay, out to Peel Castle, off the far western point of Low Furness. Eastward, it overlooks the lone green vale of Arnside, with its little tarn shining in the hollow, and beyond there is a view of Farleton Knot, and of the sands formed by the river Kier. The walls of this ancient border stronghold are of great thickness, and the small rude windows, doorways, shot-holes, and quaint fireplaces are still visible. There are no evidences of any other ancient outbuildings or defences connected with it, and, probably, as Dr. Whittaker says, "It has been merely a place of temporary retreat, in case of sudden alarm from the north, for the neighbouring inhabitants." With the exception of an old farmhouse, a little below the tower, there is no other building in all the vale of Arnside. The old name of the township was "Earnseat," from the "earn," for which it was a favourite retreat in ancient times. The district, especially about the "Knot," is famous for rare ferns, and the northern shore of that rocky height is a favourite wandering ground of the geologist. Leaving the road on the slope of "Arnside Knot," we walked through the old farm-yard below, and thence up to the tower. Within, all was ruined, and wild, and roofless, but we found the ancient winding limestone staircase sufficiently good for us to get to the top without difficulty. Here we sat down on the broad, grass-grown, ruined wall, to look about us. In spite of the beauty of the woods on "Arnside Knot," the greenness of the vale, and the fine views east and west, there was a touch of desolation in the scene, to which the mouldering tower we sat upon contributed a solemn share. In the east a train, laden with Furness ore, darted by the end of the vale, and broke the dreamy stillness with remembrances of the active world. It passed, and all was still again, except where a number of swallows skimmed the air in graceful flights between our ruined resting-place and the ground. I chanced to fling some shreds of paper from the tower, which, as they were borne away in quivering gyrations by the wind, were instantly pursued by the birds, and rarely reached the ground before they were caught by one or other of these dainty ariels, and carried off to nooks in the eaves of the old farmhouse below. One of my friends said it reminded him of the pursuit of knowledge under difficulties, and was another evidence of the growing taste for reading in these times. Another suggested that perhaps these Arnside swallows might inherit the souls of departed politicians, and were anxious to know something of the political movements of the day; and, pointing to a bird which dropped the shred he had caught in his bill, he said that one evidently didn't agree with the leading article, and therefore declined to take the paper in any further. Another thought they might have heard of the dispute about the duty, or might be in some way interested in the consumption of the article. But rumblings of distant thunder warned us that we had far to go, so we came down the stairs of the ruined tower, and began the ascent of "Arnside Knot." A good footpath leads aslant the hill, through groves of larch, spruce, and fir, whose different hues of green look very beautiful in the sunshine. About half way we left the footpath, and struck up the shingly hill-side to save time. The slope was steeper than an ordinary roof, and the shingles gave way at every step; but we toiled up, often using our hands, till we reached a green spot at the edge of the wood upon the summit. Here, among gorse bushes and tufts of ling, we found it very pleasant to rest. The view was fine from this point. At the foot of the hill lay the lone vale of Arnside, with its hoary tower standing solitarily at the head, like a worn out soldier dreaming of departed wars—and its silvery pool shining in the green hollow, the little bright eye of all the silent dell. Over the fir-clad ridge beyond we had a charming glimpse of Silverdale, and its pretty sequestered village near the sea. I understand that the sands on Silverdale shore are very fine for bathing. In this delightful dale there is a small lake called "Hawes Tarn," crowded with pike, and remarkable for its thick bed of snow-white, tiny, univalve sea shells, of fragile beauty. The waters of this tarn are said to be affected by the rise and fall of the tide. The sun was shining all around, and we had a full view of "Farleton Knot," and the picturesque limestone bridges running eastward. In a far corner of the Milnthorpe Sands, the white tower of Heversham church peeped out prettily from the green woods down by the shore; whilst in the east all the great Yorkshire hills were robed in gloom, and solemn rollings of distant thunder told that a storm was raging among them. It was a glorious sight; but cool gusts came now and then through the sunshine, and the trees on "Arnside Knot" began to talk of the coming tempest. Our old friend said that rain would certainly overtake us before the day had run by, and as a fir tree was but a riddly shelter in heavy showers, we had better go nearer the haunts of man. He pocketed his geological hammer, slung his strong wallet over his shoulder, and led on through scratchy brushwood, under the green shades that cover all the hill top, emerging on the open northern slope, from whence the view of "Whitbarrow," the shores and sands and channel of the Kent, and the distant mountains of Cumberland, is wonderfully fine. Descending to the water side, our old friend donned his spectacles, and took out his hammer again; and the two geologists wandered about the rocky shore in a trance of scientific delight, picking up many specimens interesting to them. One of these specimens I was requested to show to an eminent geologist in Manchester, whose name was familiar to them. We found some simple, substantial cheer at a little country inn, called the "Fighting Cocks," near the river side. From this place we went westward a mile or so, then up the valley of the Winster to "Castle Head," where we spent two pleasant hours in the house and grounds. From thence we crossed over "Aggerslack," down into "Lindal Lane," then up the opposite steep again, by way of "Slack Farm," right over the rocky summit of "Hampsfield Fell," descending into the old town of Cartmel, where we took tea at the "Cavendish Arms," the principal inn, which stands on the site of the ancient priory buildings, near the church. A seven mile walk in the gloaming through Cartmel park, by the woods of Holker, and partly over the Leven Sands, brought us to Ulverstone about ten at night, after twenty miles walk, just in time to get well wet by the storm which we had watched in the forenoon from the eastern edge of "Arnside Knot." In spite of this, I hardly ever had a more delightful ramble through a more finely-varied country than the one I had that day. After this passing notice of my excursion to Arnside, I will now return to my first ride to Ulverstone by rail.

Soon after the train leaves Arnside Station, the great bay begins to show itself as we rumble over the fine viaduct that crosses the river Kent, and the yellow sands of its estuary spread out on each hand. One of my fellow-travellers pointed to a lonely stork standing quietly in the midst of the sandy waste, like some weird genius of the solitude. On the other side, near the embankment, the "Old John," the oldest trading vessel of Morecambe Bay, was ashore. The low slopes near the line are richly wooded with light-hued larch, and spruce, and fir, mingling beautifully with dark green yew trees. The line now clips the rocky shore for about a mile, and we are rolling over the little river Winster, one of the boundary lines of Lancashire and Westmoreland; but, like the rest of these waters in Morecambe Bay, so changeful in its course over the sands, that yon pretty island, a little way from the shore, which looks "as quiet as a spot of sky among the evening clouds," has been known to be first in Lancashire, then in Westmoreland, and back

KENT VIADUCT.

again in Lancashire, all in a month's time, through the caprice of this little Winster, which, when the fit is on it, thus plays at hide-and-seek with the two counties. The scenery richens as we roll along. The grand bay on one side, on the other picturesque rocks and snatches of woodland, sloping to the shore, with the wild fells behind, all going by in panoramic flight. It was about low water: the sun was setting, and all that great marine wilderness, beyond which the retired sea was out of sight,—if a long line of golden light, far off, had not told its whereabouts—that sandy expanse was so still that, but for here and there a stranded boat, and a smack left aslant on the shore in the distance, it might have been a sea-beach belonging to some world unknown to man. This threshold of the mighty sea, where its children come to play, and on which so many suns have looked the grand farewell of day, was once more lighted with a glory which made the pomp of man seem poor.

This valley, on the right hand, through which the Winster flows, is a beautiful scene. The level plain, enclosed by an irregular semicircle of hills, is all land reclaimed from the sea at different times. More than four hundred acres have been added to this reclamation by the new railway line. A remarkable conical hill, thickly clothed with wood, rises from the plain, in an isolated way. This singular height is called "Castle Head," anciently, "Atterpile Castle." There is a quaint mansion in a secluded part of the grounds, and "if ever there was a house with a story, that looks like one." The sea formerly washed round the hill, and, as the old mariner at Grange told me, "it must have becu a capital place for smuggling in those days." "Castle Head" is supposed to have been a Roman settlement, or outpost of some kind, from the discovery of coins, ornaments, and other articles of Roman workmanship. About sixty years ago many curious articles were found there, among which were parts of a human skull, vertebræ, &c., teeth of buffaloes, tusks of boar, pieces of limestone, resembling hen's eggs; rings of blue rag-stone, lead, clay, and glass; ninety-five sticas of Northumbrian kings, seventy-five Roman coins, a stone, supposed to have been a mould for casting silver rings; iron ore, petrified bone, pebbles, impressions of clay, pottery, or bone, and other ancient relics. This looks as if "Castle Head" was a place of many strange stories, which have drifted into the misty past to return no more. The tenantless hall of "Castle Head" stands amongst woods and gardens at the rearward base of this lonely-looking height. The sole inhabitants of the place, at present, consist of a Scotch gardener and his family. When I visited the spot, with my two scientific friends, we wandered sometime before we met with "Sandy," till, at last, by dint of shouting—which seemed to hush into wistful stillness the lonely woods around—we roused him from one of the hothouses. He led us through the echoing rooms of the empty mansion, up to the roof, from which we had a good view of the gardens and grounds. After this we ascended, by circuitous paths, and rocky bemossed steps, terrace after terrace, to the shady plateau upon the summit of this singular hill, which certainly is suggestive of a deserted encampment. I could imagine any of the races which have had mastery in Britain occupying that commanding eminence. The views over the bay, from embowered seats and recesses on the southern edge, are very beautiful. Obliging "Sandy" was full of simple earnestness about ferns and flowers. He seemed to have little enthusiasm about anything but horticulture, except autographs, of which he showed us a curious store, collected during many years. He was quite at home in this picturesque solitude, although the place is said to be haunted, and "Thir folk i' the village o' Lindal, wha wadna walk ower't after dark for the hail estate." In the lower escarpment of rock, on the southern side, our old geological friend pointed out a place where the union of the two stratifications of slate and limestone shows distinctly. This is the only place in the district where this union is so clearly visible.

Nearly opposite the green recess in which "Castle Head" is such a singular feature of the scene, "Holme Island" stands in the bay, about two hundred yards from the railway line, and, as Spenser says, it

> "Seems so sweet and pleasant to the eye,
> That it would tempt a man to touchen there."

Less than half a century since, this island was little more than a bare rock—a lone domain of wind and wave, and birds that love the sea. Within that time, however, it has, at immense expense, been converted into a perfect marine paradise. Though not much more than ten acres in extent, the gardens and grounds are so tastefully varied that a man may ramble an hour or two about it and still find himself in a new scene—still meet with "something rich and strange"—and, in some parts, the little landscape is so artfully natural in appearance that he might forget it was the result of man's taste and enterprise. On the western side of the island, a white limestone building, perfectly modelled after the temple of Vesta, looks out westward over the bay; and, in sheltered nooks, rock-hewn stairs lead down to sand-banks so smooth, so gently-swelling and secluded, that fair Sabrina might sit there

> "Under the cool translucent wave
> Her bright hair knitting,"

free from fear of intrusion. The grounds and gardens are rich in plants and flowers of the rarest description, from all parts of the world. The house is shadily situated, about the middle of the island, among fine trees and tasteful grounds.

From the highest points and openings in the shades of "Holme Island"—that sylvan gem of the waters—the views are wildly beautiful or solemnly grand, whichever way we turn. Far out, off the extreme north-western shore of the bay, the massive ruins of Peel Castle—that ancient stronghold of the abbots of Furness—stand mouldering in wild isolation among the waves.

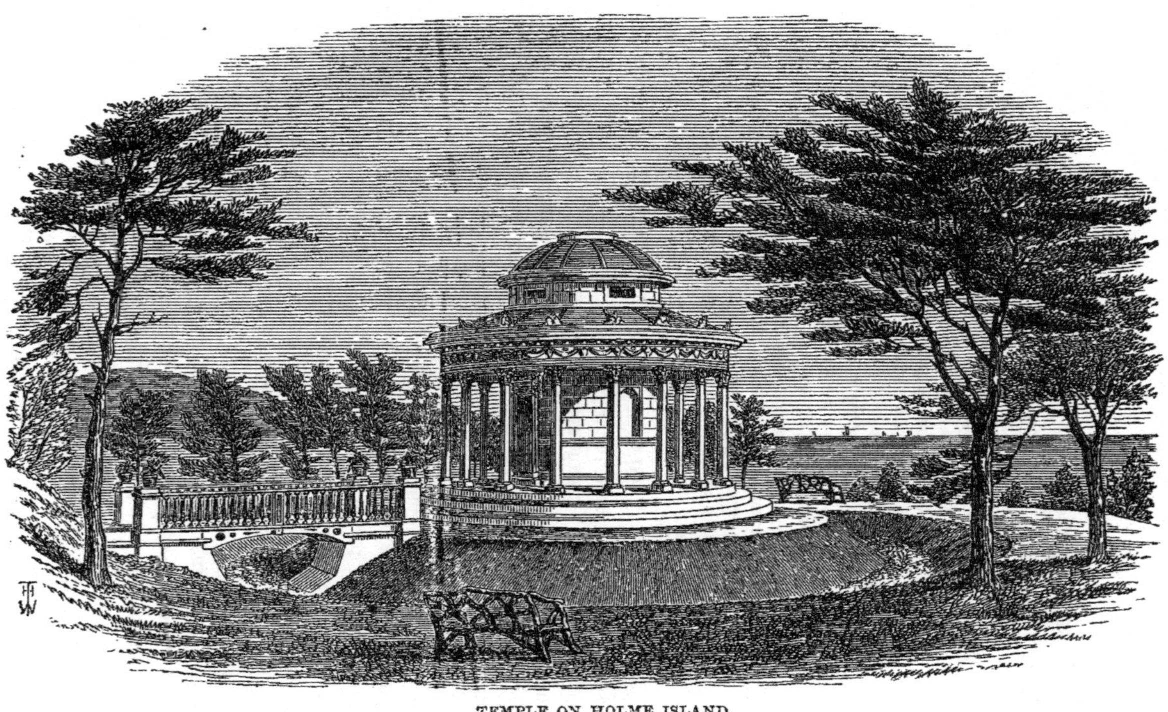

TEMPLE ON HOLME ISLAND.

They have done with the marauding Scot, the pomp of prelates, and the din of war; and now, all silent and unsentinelled, they glide majestically into the wastes of time. Left to the washing waves and whistling winds—a crumbling shelter of the seabird—

> "The empty ruins lapsed again
> Into nature's wide domain,
> Sow themselves with seed and grain,
> As day and night and day go by."

Leaving this ruined fortress, the eye travels along the low fertile shores on which Aldingham Castle and village, now washed away, once stood near the sea. The bold peaks of Higher Furness in the rearward of the scene. The village of Bardsea, Conishead Priory, the town of Ulverstone, and the beautiful estuary of the Leven, are all hidden from "Holme Island" by the promontory of Cartmel; but on the north, it commands a fine view of the most picturesque part of the Cartmel shore, with the tops of its woody fells standing against the sky, like the wild outlines of a petrified tempest. Looking east, the fells between Lancaster and Kendal, and, beyond these, Ingleborough, and other Yorkshire hills, may be seen. Southward, and immediately opposite the island, is "Arnside Knot," with its fir-grove crown. Farther south, Warton Crags rise up, and villas and white mansions gleam among the thickly-wooded lower slopes, till Silverdale Point seems to shoot into the bay, like a great dark needle. Beyond this, the green ridges of Bolton-le-Sands, Carnforth, Hest Bank, Heysham, Poulton-le-Sands, and the "Sunderland Shoulder," hide the estuary of the Lune, "that to old Loncaster his name doth lend," of which river Michael Drayton says so cheerily:—

> "For salmon me excels; and for this name of Lun,
> That I am christened by, the Britons it begun,
> Which fulness doth import of waters still increase
> To Neptune lowting low, when christal Lune doth cease;
> And Conder coming in conducts her by the hand,
> Till lastly she salutes the Point of Sunderland,
> And leaves our dainty Lune to Amphitrite's care.
> So blyth and bonny now the lads and lasses are,
> That ever and anon the bagpipe up doth blow;
> Cast in a gallant round about the hearth they go,
> And every village smokes at wakes with lusty cheer,
> Then hey, they cry, for Lun, and hey for Lancashire,
> That one high hill was heard to tell it to his brother."

All this, however, gives but a very imperfect idea of the great extent and variety of view from "Holme Island." The shoreward scenes opposite are very beautiful.

CHAPTER II.

It is the shout of the coming foe,
Ride, ride for thy life, Sir John;
But still the waters deeper grew,
The wild sea foam rushed on.

Old Ballad.

A LITTLE beyond "Holme Island," and about half-way between Carnforth and Ulverstone, the train stops at the pretty seaside village of Grange. It looks very inviting from the railway, but not till one is in it can they fairly see how pretty it is, and how fine the views are from its higher parts. From the rail it looks a cluster of gardens and white limestone houses scattered about the undulent lower slopes of "Yewbarrow," a craggy wooded height which fills the immediate background. It matters very little where you build a house in Grange, it is sure to have a pleasant outlook, and is never in the way of its neighbour; for the land over which the dwellings are so picturesquely dribbled about is all fertile dingles, and knolls, and nest-like nooks, mixed with bloomy orchards, flower gardens, and scattered tufts of wood; and there are several mansions thereabout, whose green shades and ornamental grounds give a park-like tone to the skirts of the village. The church, with its tiny "heaven-pointing" spire, stands on a green eminence at the head of the village. Near the church, as usual, there is a comfortable old inn. The open space in front of "The Crown," commands a good view of the eastern part of the bay, with the Yorkshire hills behind, and all the picturesque fells and wooded shores on the Lancaster side. Grange, though not unknown to fame among lovers of nature and wanderers to the sea, has, like the rest of Cartmel, been peculiarly secluded by its position. The Lancaster and Ulverstone line now runs by the foot of the village, bringing it into direct communication with the main lines from the south. Before the railway was made, the tide washed the garden walls of the village.

GRANGE.

As I walked about the open elevated ground in front of the "Crown," looking at the bay and the hills, I asked several questions of two or three villagers who were lounging about. They eyed me from head to foot, wondering where I came from, and what I had to do with their hills and dales; at last, settling in their own minds that I must be a strange land-surveyor, preparing for fresh changes in that part of the country. I think the civil old landlord himself began to be puzzled, for, beckoning to a stalwart young man, who stood down in the village-street with a bundle of papers in his hand, he said—"That's the man for ye. He's read a deeal o' books. He knaas summat abaat ivvery thing, nearly; an' he knaas mair abaat Grange, I sud think, than onybody at's in it." I found him an enthusiastic entomologist and ornithologist, and a very unassuming, intelligent man, of manly manners. We sat down in the "Crown" chatting, and listening whilst "Aad Billy," a blind fiddler, who lives by scattering music among the kind-hearted folk of Cartmel Fells, played "Scots wha hae wi' Wallace bled," and "Bannocks o' bear meal, bannocks o' barley." The old man beat time with his foot, and accompanied his instrument with a curious croon, which made up in quaintness for what it lacked in harmony. I could not help thinking, as he sat there, that a country village without a blind fiddler is wanting in a valuable feature of human interest. Leaving "Aad Billy" at the end of "O'er Bogie," my friend proposed that we should go to the top of "Yewbarrow," the hill at the rear of the village, from the summit of which he said the views were magnificent. As we went out at the head of the village by a shady road, he opened the gate of a small enclosed knoll, on the right hand, saying, "Stop, my workshop is in here. We'll peep at it, if you like, before we go up." In the centre of this enclosure there was a rude, round hut, built of limestone, something like a large summer-house. On entering, I found myself in a little museum, filled with strange birds, and carefully arranged glass cases of rare shells and insects. Against the wall hung a broken skeleton head and horns of the Irish elk, which had been found in the neighbouring sands, a few years ago. In one corner was reared a large slab of red sandstone, from Storton, in Cheshire, on which were plainly imprinted the footsteps of some antediluvian creature; he thought it was the *plesiasaurus*. The place was full of curiosities; and I noticed a live wood owl, in a cage outside, with its large, lustrous eyes, blinking in the sunshine. Leaving this little sanctum of science, we went through the shady grounds of "Yewbarrow Lodge," and thence, by rocky, sinuous paths to the summit of "Yewbarrow." This hill takes its name from the yew tree, for the growth of which it is remarkable, and from "barrow," a cairn or burial place. Here I was glad to sit down and look round, for I was out of wind, and the view had grown grander as we rose. Morecambe and a great extent of its shores were full in sight, the slopes and lowlands all beauty and fertility, all above and in the distance wild and majestic. My friend told me that, on a favourable day, the town of Lancaster was almost as distinctly in sight as the houses at the foot of the hill; but he surprised me more by saying that all the great, ivy-clad, limestone rocks upon the summit of "Yewbarrow," were unmistakably water-worn, that is, worn by the action of the sea. The village lay under the eye, as clearly as a map or model on a table. We could see all its houses, perching or nestling in picturesque confusion, among straggling gardens and bloomy nooks. We could see all its mansions, with their rich grounds, and woods now spreading out the bright green of spring in the sunshine; its white roads and bye lanes, winding through orchards, and under over-lapping trees, about the green knolls and dingles, and lacing the land with lines of ever-varying loveliness. Grange is no less pleasant in its own quiet beauty, and in the scenery about it, than in the salubrity of its climate, which is said to rival that of the southern coast of England. In spring, its average temperature is higher than that of any other place in the north of England. In summer, the heat is tempered by the saline breeze. Beautifully seated on this lower slope of "Yewbarrow," it is sheltered on the north and west by the green hills, and its natural charms are heightened by the never-palling witcheries of the changeful sea. Artists, and other curious children of nature, who love to go about the world "spyin' fancies," as country folk quaintly call it, would find its neighbourhood full of interest.

It was a beautiful sight; and, as I descended the hill, by another route, to meet the train, I resolved that, if possible, it should not be long before I looked upon that peaceful nest again.

The grandest height near Grange is "Hampsfell," at the rear of "Yewbarrow." Whosoever desires to see that country well, ought to ascend "Hampsfell," at sunrise or sunset, on a fine day, and he may look upon a scene of such magnificence as is rarely met with in any land. For those who are not strong, a carriage road leads up the south side of Eggerslack wood, nearly to the summit of the fell; but the sturdy pedestrian should go out at the lower end of Grange, and up the narrow, romantic glen, called "Lindal Lane," till he comes to a farmhouse called "Slack," on the left hand side of the road. This shady gorge is a little fairy-land of woodland beauty in summer time. After crossing the yard of Slack farm, a rough footpath leads up through plantations of larch and spruce; and coppice woods of oak and hazel, sprinkled, now and then, with the glittering birch—that silver-robed lady of the woods—the beech, the ash "for nothing ill," the alder, and the dark green yew, "obedient to the bender's will." These woods, which are carefully cultivated for "bobbin wood," hoops, wicker-work, and other purposes, are great sources of employment to the people around. As the traveller winds through the sylvan scene, by changeful pleasure upward led, he meets with glimpses of the sea, gleaming through the southward trees;

and there is many a nook of the mountain path where he may sit in cool shadow, listening to the wild birds which fill all the woods with their tuneful rejoicings. Emerging from this leafy screen, he finds rocky, unshaded moorlands, stretching upward still, in silent desolation. Great picturesque masses of limestone crop out from the heathery waste, their ragged crevices beautiful with plumy ferns. There is still a rude pathway to the summit, but, for a good walker, "Th' Crow-gate" across the moor will be more interesting. At last, the top of a square, squat limestone tower appears on the distant height. This is "Hampsfell Hospice," a modern erection, built by a former pastor of Cartmel parish, for the shelter and entertainment of wanderers over the fell. As he draws nearer this little benevolent coronet of lonely "Hampsfell," mountain and vale, and land and sea, expand so gloriously, that he cannot but halt now and then to gaze around with wonder and delight. Inside the tower there are stone seats, and a good fire-place, for which the heather around affords ready and abundant kindling. Upon the walls are wooden tablets, inscribed with verses allusive to the scenery, and the purpose of the building. From these I copied the following:—

"This hospice has an open door,
Welcome alike to rich and poor;
A roomy seat for young and old,
Where they may screen them from the cold;
Three windows that command a view,
To north, to west, and southward too;
A flight of steps requiring care;
A roof that shews a prospect rare;
Mountain and vale you thence survey,—
The winding streams and noble bay.
The sun at noon the shadow hides
Along the east and westward sides.
A lengthened chain holds guard around,
To keep the cattle from the ground.
Kind reader, freely take your pleasure,
But do no mischief to my treasure!"

From the roof of this "Hospice" the views are indeed glorious, both in variety of character and extent of range. Fertile, peace-breathing valleys; old castles, and churches, and quaint hamlets and towns,—eloquent relics of past history; lonely glens, rich parks, and forest steeps; picturesque homesteads, in pleasant nooks of shelter; beautiful estuaries; the fresh blue bay, bleak brown moorlands; wild craggy fells; and storm-worn mountains, each different in height and form,—the grand old guardians of the magnificent scene. Beginning with Peel Castle, in the sea-washed west, the eye wanders over solemn Black Coombe, and Druid Swinstead, Fletcher Fell, Stoneshead, and all the Coniston range, in which the bold round peak of the "Old Man" is the most familiar mark. Then come Langdale Pikes, Scaw Fell, Great End, Bow Fell, part of Skiddaw, shewing itself beyond the gap of Dunmail; then "the dark brow of the mighty Helvellyn," monarch of all that wonderful land of beautiful waters, rises up majestically above the green valley of St. John. Looking eastward, we see the pleasant vale of the Kent, with its fine estuary; the woodland shores of Milnthorpe; the grand crags of Whitbarrow and Farleton, with kindred limestone ridges stretching out beyond. Farther eastward the hills of Yorkshire rise in the blue sky. In the south, over Arnside, Silverdale, and Warton, we have the fells and green lowlands of the Lancaster side; ridge after ridge then hides the Lune and the Wyre, till the masts and lighthouse of Fleetwood shew themselves far out to seaward. If the day be fine, the mountains of Wales, the Isle of Man, and even the coast of Ireland may sometimes be seen. It is a glorious combination of land and sea; but, perhaps, the most charming bit of all the landscape is the valley of Cartmel, just at the western foot of Hampsfell. The little town, nestling round its venerable church, looks so near that one might almost expect to hear some sounds of life arise therefrom; but it is as still down there in the middle of the sunlit vale as if it was only the quaint centre-piece in the pattern of a green carpet.

I feel that what is here written gives but an imperfect idea of the wonderful prospects commanded by Hampsfell; and I can only add that no traveller, who has opportunity, and cares for the glories of nature, ought to go by that mountain unclimbed. I have noticed, after ascending some of the highest points of that district, that although the same objects may chance to be seen from several heights, yet the points of view are so different that in each case we get a new picture.

In the neighbourhood of Grange there are several mansions and houses of considerable interest, such as "Abbot Hall," "Hampsfield Hall." "Witherslack Hall"—a fine old house, formerly belonging to the Earls of Derby; "Cark Hall," "Bigland Hall," "Merlewood," and "Holker Hall," the favourite seat of the Duke of Devonshire, with its noble park sloping down to picturesque cliffs of mountain limestone and old red sandstone. Holker park contains many remarkable trees, of much greater size than is common so near the sea.

The distance from Grange to Newby Bridge, at the foot of Windermere, is six miles. The road thither winds out at the lower end of Grange, between the woody heights of Aggerslack and Blawith, and up the beautiful glen called "Lindal Lane." An omnibus runs twice a day in summer between these points, through the villages of Lindal and Newton. The village of Lindal, about two miles from Grange, is worth going a long way to look at. It is not only picturesque in itself, but is picturesquely situated among scenes of singular beauty, and commands an enchanting peep of the bay, with a view of the rich vale in which "Castle Head" is such a singular feature. The whole six miles ride to Newby Bridge through Cartmel Fells is full of interest to anyone who can enjoy the contrast of peaceful fertility overlooked by craggy wildness, which he will pass through on the way.

Quaint Cartmel, the market town of the sequestered district which bears its name, is little more than two miles north of Grange—a pleasant walk over the hills on a fine day. Its noble old priory is the only conventual church in Lancashire which escaped mutilation after the dissolution of the monasteries. This escape arose from its being partly the parish church, as as well as the church of the priory. About three miles from this town, and about the same from Grange, is the famous "Holy Well of Cartmel"—a fine medicinal spring, which is a great attraction in the summer months. Its waters are celebrated for the cure of gout, stone, and cutaneous diseases. For many years past the miners employed in the Alston Moor Lead Mines, being liable to certain diseases arising from the nature of their labours, have made annual pilgrimage to the village of Kent's Bank, near here, in order to have the benefit of Cartmel's "Holy Well." Cartmel is a settlement of great antiquity. Camden says of the district, that "in 677, Egfrid, King of Northumbria, gave St. Cuthbert the land, and all the Britons in it." "In 1188," according to Baines, "the foundation of a priory for canons regular of St. Augustine was laid by William Mareschal, the elder, Earl of Pembroke." His charter concludes with these words:—"This house I have founded for the increase of our holy religion, giving and granting to it every kind of liberty that heart can conceive, or the mouth utter; and whoever shall in any way infringe upon these immunities, or injure the said priory, may he incur the curse of God, of the blessed Virgin Mary, and all other saints, as well as my particular malediction." This priory was enriched by many grants and donations of pontiffs and princes, and many "offerings of the faithful." The town is situated in a vale watered by two streams, one running north and the other south. Between these streams stands the fine old conventual church, with its curious belfry rising from the central tower, a square inscribed within a square diagonal to its base. Of course, there is a tradition connected with the foundation of Cartmel Priory. It seems that nearly seven hundred years ago, a number of foreign monks, wandering about the country in search of a settlement, somehow found their way into this, then, dense forest wild. They were preparing to build their church upon a hill-top in the neighbourhood, when a voice spoke to them out of the air, saying: "Not there; but in a valley between two rivers, where the one runs north and the other south." It seems unfortunate that the voice should neglect to tell them where that valley was, as they happened to be so near it at the time. But it was so; for these homeless fathers wandered, after that, all over the north of England, in fruitless search, until they found the place, at last, near the very hill where they first heard "the voice in the air." Here, on an island of hard ground between these singular streams, they bullt the Priory of Cartmel, and dedicated it to St. Mary. They also built a small chapel on the hill, where they heard the voice, and they dedicated it to St. Bernard. The chapel is now gone, but the hill is called "St. Bernard's Mount" to this day.

Going from a place like Manchester into this little monastic town is almost like going to bed, or sinking into an antiquarian dream, all is so quaint and quiet. The market-place is a square of old-fashioned houses, with the fish stones near the middle. This old market-place looked so drowsy when I saw it that it seemed astonished if anybody walked across it. On one side, an ancient gateway leads into a cloistral old street, in which the principal inn is situated. This gateway is a relic of the original buildings connected with the priory. There are inns of more imposing appearance, but I met with kind attention and good cheer at the King's Arms, near the bridge, where I spent a pleasant hour among some hungry wood-cutters, who had been at work all day in the fells. Following the advice of a former traveller in Cartmel, I had inquired of a man with a red nose, who happened to be leaning on the bridge, where I could get a good glass of ale, and he directed me to this house. I found the place filled with a very cheerful aroma; and, in a few minutes, I got so thick with the hungry woodcutters, who were waiting for their evening meal, that I was invited to join them at an immense dish of savoury "lobscouse," prepared by the handsome, good-tempered landlady. Judging by the alacrity with which the dish was emptied, I should say that every stomach there was in good order; and I only hope these jolly woodmen had not miscalculated my capacity when they invited me to the feast,—for, simple as the fare was, the feast was fine. We finished off with oatcake, and butter and cheese, and a glorious dish of crisp water-cresses—the whole seasoned with a good deal of hearty fun, which is not the worst part of the best meal a man can eat. From this house the landlord directed me to an old building, occupied as a saddler's shop, in the opposite corner of the square. Here I found the parish clerk, William Lancaster, who kindly took me through the church and up to the top of the central tower.

The walls of the choir and transept of this old church belong to the first erection; the windows are of later date. There is a noble east window, 48 feet high, containing some fine stained glass. On the north side of the proper choir is a narrow chapel, anciently called the "Piper's Choir;" and on the south side what is called the "Town Choir," which has two stone seats for the officiating priests. This is supposed to have been anciently the parish church. There are 26 ancient stalls in the choir, with their grotesquely-carved *misereres*, all in perfect condition. There are many ancient monumental decorations in this church; but the most remarkable is a magnificent monument of the Harrington family, under an arched canopy. In the old library I was shown some rare and curious books, among which were the following:—"The Second Part of the Faerie Queene, containing the Fourth, Fifth, and Sixth Bookes. By Ed. Spencer. Printed at London, for William Ponsonby, 1596." A folio copy of "Fox's Book of Martyrs," in black letter, 1610. A black-letter Bible, in six vols, printed at Basle, in 1502. A quarto copy of the works of Thomas Aquinas, in black letter, printed at Venice, in

1506. A quaint little volume entitled "Apophthegemes New and Old, collected by the Right Honourable Francis Lo. Verulam, Viscount St. Alban, 1625." The Ancient Parish Register of Cartmel for the last 300 years. As we came out the clerk pointed to the Duke of Devonshire's pew; and I found, everywhere, that his grace, and the family altogether, have the right goodwill of the people of Cartmel. After a parting stroll by twilight round the noble old church, and its calm, quaint, pastoral town, just as the stars began to struggle with declining day, I took the lonely road to Grange, through Allithwaite, a rude village, whose inhabitants, like those of Cark and Flookborough, live mainly by fishing and cockling upon the sands.

These villages consist principally, in each case, of one straggling street of humble cottages; and, though there is not much attraction in their outward appearance, considerable interest attaches to the peculiar way of human life therein. Some idea of the fishery on this shore may be had from the fact that, in addition to flook, plaice, salmon, and other fish, there is sometimes as much as one thousand tons of cockles sent from Cark, in one season, principally to the manufacturing towns of Lancashire. Cockles are found in large beds, called "skeers." The fish is buried about an inch below the surface, and its place is known by two little holes in the sand, called "eyes;" from thence the cockler whips out the fish with a kind of three-pronged bent fork, called a "craam." Although these cocklers generally belong to the poorest class of people, no quarrels take place among them on the sands. This arises from a firm belief that if ever they quarrel upon the sands, the cockles would leave that place with the next tide.

It is in these three fishing villages that the lead-miners of Northumberland and other visitors to the "Holy Well" take up their quarters, but chiefly, I believe, at Flookborough, where there is comfortable accommodation to be had. Flookborough, as its name indicates, was formerly a market town, holding a charter granted to the Prior of Cartmel, by Edward the First. After the dissolution, this charter was removed to Cartmel. The first part of the name may or may not come from the fish so common on these shores,—but I heard that a certain dignitary of the church, once visiting there, inquired of a villager how many souls (soles) there were in the place, and the man replied, "Well, I dinnet justly knaa; but here's a terrible decal o' flooks abaat."

The country between Grange and the Leven sands, about five miles, is very interesting. Soon after the train leaves Grange, we run through a rocky cutting, which brings us to Cark station, two miles from Cartmel, to which town an omnibus runs daily in summer time. The line then passes Kent's Bank, with its pleasantly-situated villas, near which "Abbot Hall," a modest, modern mansion, stands in that green corner of the shore, on the site of an old house, said to have belonged to a slyly-jovial prelate of the olden time. Leaving this place, we run about two miles by the promontory of Humphrey Head, and then begin to cross Ulverstone sands. The scenery about Humphrey Head is a fine mixture of the bold and the beautiful; and the country around is full of picturesque rambles. Up in its grand yew-crowned cliffs there is a remarkable cave, believed by the natives to be an abode of fairies. The famous "Holy Well" is on the western shore of this fine promontory.

Upon a low fertile level, between Grange and Humphrey Head, a little grey ruin stands near the line. This is Wraysholme Tower, formerly a fortified house, belonging to the knightly family of Harrington, of Aldingham Castle, in Low Furness. The Saxon town of Aldingham belonged to this family in 1346. Both town and castle have long since been swept away by the sea.

There is more than one legend connected with this ancient tower. The following, called "The Last Wolf," is given in the "Remains of John Briggs," editor of the old Lonsdale Magazine. It appears from the tradition, which has been put into spirit-stirring verse a few years ago, by an anonymous writer, that in the proud old days of Wraysholme, Sir Edgar Harrington had sworn to hunt down the last wolf "in England's spacious realm," whose haunt was the woody height of Humphrey Head, and whose prey the flocks and herds of Wraysholme. On the eve of the chase Sir Edgar held a mighty carousal at the tower, among his retainers and noble guests. During the feast he swore that the last wolf should "grace the conqueror's helm," and, also, that—

"Whoe'er that wolf should quell,
Should have his fair niece for a bride,
And half his lands as well."

The orphan lady Adela, old Sir Edgar's ward, with jet black hair of glossy sheen, and bright hazel eyes, was beloved of all the country round; but her heart and troth were with a gallant young knight of the name of Harrington, Sir Edgar's son, who, having fled to shun his father's wrath, was supposed to be dead in foreign lands. He seems, however, to have turned up at this great hunting feast just in time, after winning honour against the swarthy Saracen, disguised under the title of Sir John Delisle, in whom, nevertheless, the old retainers of Wraysholme see that—

"A long lost wanderer meets their sight,
Whate'er his name be now."

But, as usual, there are cross purposes in this old tale of love and chivalry, for Layburne, another brave knight, and the friend of Sir Edgar, sits by the board, close suitor for the fair lady, though "from her soul abhorred." The night drives on in song and jest, and brimming goblets,

"Till late, with plenteous cheer oppressed,
And foaming tankards drowned,
The revellers retire to rest,
And silence sinks around."

At break of day old Hubert's horn wakes the sleepers to a mighty hunting.

> "Full threescore riders mount with speed,—
> Amidst them Layburne strides
> A gallant steed of Flemish breed,
> That well his weight abides.
>
> "Whilst mounted on an Arab white,
> Of figure light and free,
> Rides young Delisle, the stranger knight,
> All wrapt in mystery."

The huntsman leads the gallant company up to the wolf's covert on Humphrey Head. The dogs get the track of their grisly prey, and a brave chase begins, over Kirkhead and Holker to Newby Bridge, where they swim the "Leven's brawling flood." On, through woodland glen, and over wild hill they go, in clamorous dash, till the "grey beast" finds brief shelter in the recesses of Coniston Old Man. Here the hunters breathe; but their hounds are staunch, and their horses good as ever broke cover or dashed through a wood; the dogs are on the track again like grim death; away by Esthwaite, and on to the green shores of Windermere, where the panting savage takes the water at one bold plunge, "and leaves his foes behind." The rival knights, Layburne and Delisle, follow, "foremost of the dripping train," and win the eastern side of the lake. Two tireless bloodhounds keep the scent, and the chase continues along the shore to "craggy Gummershaw,"

> "Then turns aside to Witherslack,
> Where Winster's waters range,
> And thence to shingly Aggerslack,
> And sand-surveying Grange."

The doomed brute now makes with the instinct of despair for his old shelter on Humphrey Head, but as mild evening sinks upon the scene, the fatal hounds are on his track—and he is driven madly towards a wild chasm,

> "Begirt by rock on every side,
> That slopes in shade away."

Wolf and dogs rush o'er the steep. Layburne's horse starts back from the awful chasm; but impetuous Delisle spurs on, and his fiery steed sweeps to destruction down the shrouded crag like a flash of lightning—

> "The shingles in its headlong course
> With rattling din give way,
> The hazels snap beneath its force,
> The mountain savins sway."

At this terrible crisis the fair Adela chances to be pacing the hollow glen on her light palfrey, when the wolf appears in sight, and "bares his glistening teeth."

> "Her eyes are closed in mortal dread,
> And e'er a look they steal,
> The wolf and Arab both lie dead,
> And scathless stands Delisle.

"Full promptly from the slaughtered prey,
He plucks the reeking spear,
And cries 'Oh, beauteous Adela,
Behold thy true love here!'"

Sir Edgar now appears, and discovering in Delisle his lost son, welcomes him affectionately, and gives him the bride of his heart. By blessed hap the Prior of Cartmel is on his way "to drink at the Holy Well," and he consents to perform the marriage ceremony at once in the neighbouring cavern.

"And hence that cave on Humphrey Hill,
Where these fair deeds befell,
Is called Sir Edgar's chapel still,
As hunters wot full well,

"And still that holy fount is there,
To which the Prior came;
And still it boasts its virtues rare,
And bears its ancient name.

"And long on Wraysholme's lattice light
A wolf's head might be traced,
In honour of the redcross knight,
Who bore it for his crest.

"In Cartmel church his grave is shown,
And o'er it, side by side,
All graved in stone, lies brave Sir John,
And Adela his bride."

Such is the legend of "The Last Wolf," connected with this ruined tower of Wraysholme, the ancient abode of the Harringtons of Aldingham, in Low Furness. I find that, forty years ago, the place was sheltered by clumps of old trees. These are now gone, and the tower is a mere outhouse to the neighbouring farmstead.

Cark is the nearest station to Holker, the Duke of Devonshire's Cartmel seat. Holker Hall belongs to the middle of the sixteenth century, when it was the residence of a branch of the ancient family of Preston, of Preston Patrick, in Westmoreland. About a century ago this beautiful estate came into the possession of the Cavendish family. The park is full of rich sylvan landscapes, and it contains many noble trees, and trees of very rare kinds. There are delightful walks on the woodland heights behind the park, which command good views of Leven water, Thurston Vale, the mountains at the head of Windermere, and the Coniston range.

When the train clears Humphrey Head, the banks of the Leven estuary open beautifully in sight. Wild, rich-hued limestone crags straggle up the north-east side, under overhanging woods, and the low shore is all fertile undulations. The bold railway mole now crosses Ulverstone Sands, and we rumble over a lofty viaduct, where the broad Leven rolls wild and turbid underneath, as if glad to escape from this daring evidence of man's enterprise, to the uncontrollable ocean beyond. The views from the line as we cross these sands are peculiarly fine, for this estuary is perhaps the most

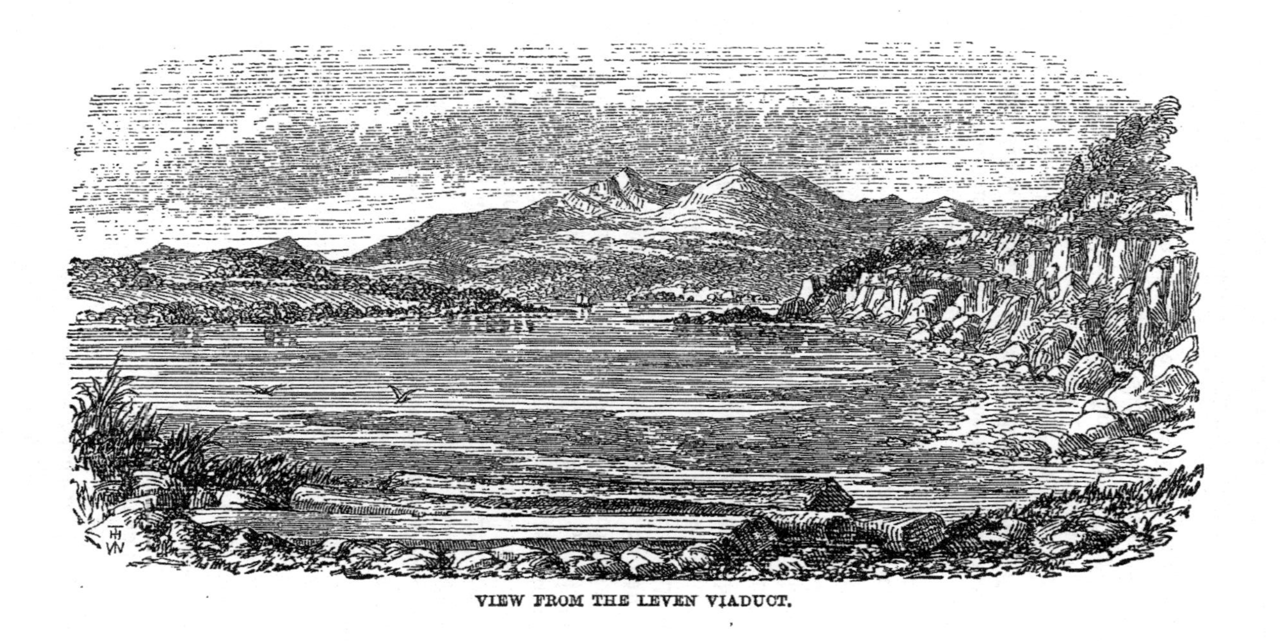

VIEW FROM THE LEVEN VIADUCT.

picturesque of any in Morecambe Bay. Westward, Birkrigg rises above the rich woods and glades of Conishead Priory. A little westward we see the white village of Sandside, opposite to which, about a mile from the shore, is that interesting little isle of prayer, called "Chapel Island," with its old ruined chantry hidden in the trees. Behind Sandside, the grey smoke of Ulverstone hovers above the valley at the foot of "Hoad Hill." The traveller may know this hill by the lighthouse-shaped monument on the top. Further along the shore there is a little cluster of shipping at the port of Ulverstone. The low grounds beyond are, first great tracts of yellow sand, then pleasant holms and valleys; behind these, woody uplands and lofty moors filling the rear of the landscape. The extreme northward view of the estuary is bounded by a great cluster of Cartmel fells, rising peak after peak. Looking eastward, the shore is a beautiful combination of rock and wildwood, with the great ridge of Hampsfell peeping over the promontory of Humphrey Head.

The Ulverstone sands are considered more dangerous than those on the Lancaster side. Mr. Baines, speaking of the old route over this estuary, says:—"The track is from Holker Hall to Plumpton Hall, keeping Chapel Island a little to the left; and the mind of a visitor is filled with a mixture of awe and gratitude, when, in a short time after he has traversed this estuary, almost dry-shod, he beholds the waters advancing into the bay, and bearing stately vessels towards the harbour of Ulverstone, over the very path which he has so recently trodden." The Priory of Conishead was anciently charged with the cost of guides across this estuary. So dangerous were these sands considered, that on "Chapel Island," about a mile west of the line, the old monks of Furness built the small chapel, where prayers were daily offered "for the safety of the souls of such as crossed the sands with the morning tide." There are still some remains of this ancient chapel, which gave its name to the island; and, though "long years have darkened into time" since the prayers of the church were regularly heard there, no man walks about the shades of this little seaworn solitude without feeling that something of the solemn interest of its ancient associations lingers with it still. The island is now a favourite resort of pleasure seekers, who cross at low water from the village of Sandside, about a mile distant—and, even in that short distance, sometimes meet with disaster. The three miles over Leven sands must have been destructively dangerous, for, "according to a petition from the Abbot of Furness, in 19 Ed. 2, the number of sixteen at one time, and six more at another, were sacrificed in this way; and in order to eschew the great mortality of the people of Furness on passing the sands at ebb of tide, he prayed that he should have a view of frankpledge and a coroner of his own; for everywhere," he says, "it would be the salvation of one soul at least."

The train is now quitting the sands, and we draw near to Ulverstone town. Long strings of carriages go by heavily laden with the rich iron ore

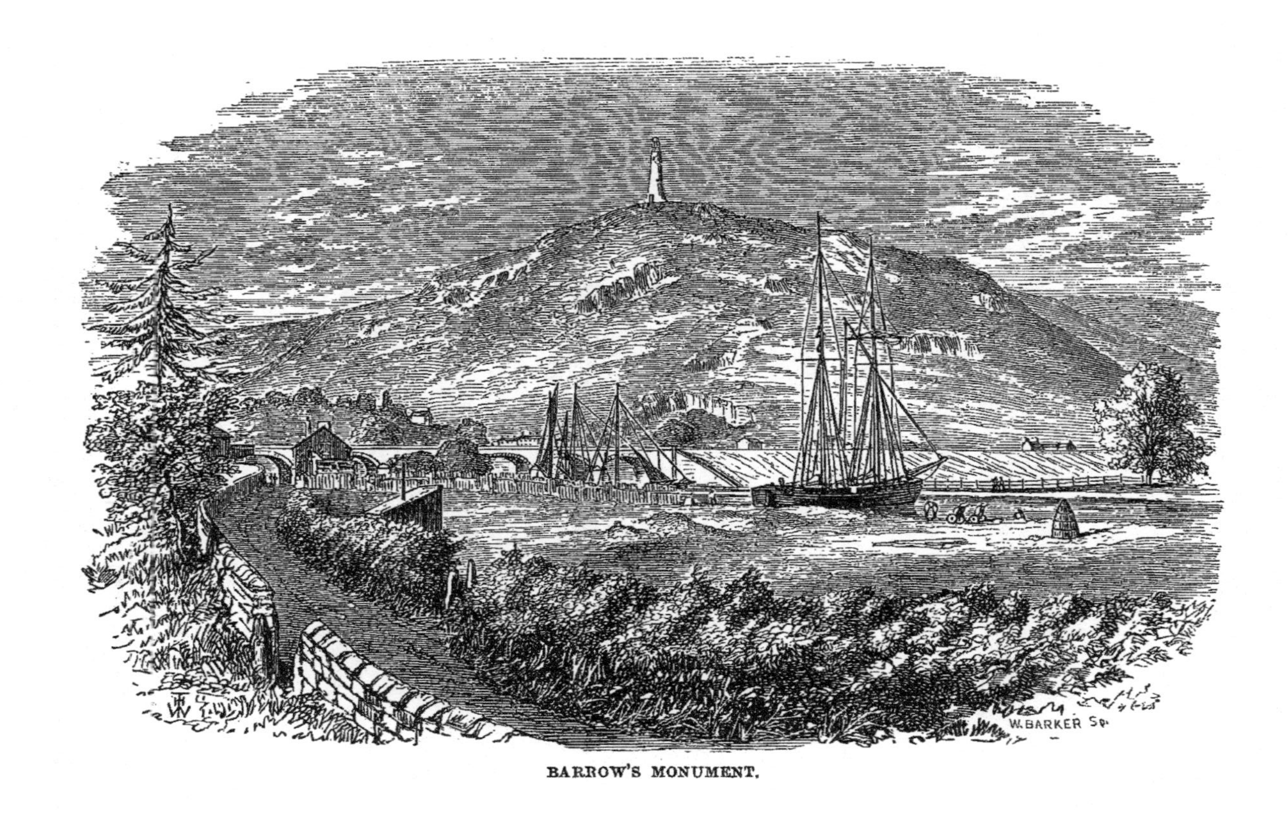

BARROW'S MONUMENT.

of Furness. I was told that the mines of this district now produce between seven and eight hundred thousand tons of the finest ore in England every year. Thirty years ago, old Captain Barrow, of Ulverstone, carried all the iron ore got in Furness in one small vessel. This Captain Barrow was cousin to Sir John Barrow, late secretary to the Admiralty, whose monument stands on the top of "Hoad," the great round hill, at the right hand side of the line as we run over the railway bridge towards Ulverstone. Sir John was born of very humble parentage, in a little cottage at Dragley Beck, near this town.

BIRTHPLACE OF SIR JOHN BARROW, AT DRAGLEY BECK.

CHAPTER III.

"About me round I saw
Hill, dale, and shady woods, and sunny plains,
And liquid lapse of murmuring streams; by these
Creatures that lived, and moved, and walked, or flew,
Birds on the branches warbling; all things smiled;
With fragrance and with joy my heart o'erflowed."
MILTON.

The view of Ulverstone and the country about it, as seen from the high road near the station, is very picturesque. The town is pleasantly situated in a vale, on the shores of the Leven estuary, among the hills of Low Furness; and it stands at convenient distances from so many points of interest that I took up head quarters at the well-known Sun Hotel, in the market place. From hence I made daily excursions into the neighbourhood; and one of my first rambles was to Swarthmoor, about a mile from the town. Swarthmoor Hall was, for many years, the residence of George Fox, founder of the Society of Friends. Leaving Ulverstone by the south road, about two hundred yards past the railway station, a bye-path leads over the fields on the right hand a little way, then down into a shady dell, through which a clear rivulet plays its moody music, running out of sight again at the south end, under thick, low-lapping branches, which gaze into it and dally with its silvery ripples, as if in love with this limpid minstrel, whose song softens into silence in the woods beyond. This quiet dell is a fairy chapel of sylvan beauty, where the ceaseless hymn of nature is seldom disturbed by other sounds. In the deepest part of the hollow, an old stone bridge, shaded by tall trees, crosses the stream; from thence a rugged footpath climbs the opposite fields, and in about a quarter of a mile leads close by the rear of a hoary pile of stone outhouses of rude appearance. The road may be miry, but whoever he be that goes that way, in rain or fair weather, let him linger there a breathing while, for the old house in front of these buildings is Swarthmoor Hall, the residence of George Fox. On my first visit, I wandered about some time before I could find any human creature astir. A contemplative charm seemed to lie upon all around. The house is a large, irregular,

Elizabethan building, with nothing grand about it, save the impressive memories of the great reformer who dwelt in it two centuries ago. The doorways are small; some of the windows are built up; and it has altogether a bald appearance, considering its size and former importance. But the home of the persecuted puritan still looks over those quiet fields with a kind of ascetic solemnity, as if it was mingling dreams of the past with a patient waiting for the result of slow decay. I wandered about

SWARTHMOOR HALL.

the rough, cattle-trodden yard, among mire, and straw, and farming-gear, yet all was still, except a few ducks dabbling in a muddy pool, and a peaceful dog that roamed about the outhouses, regardless of my presence. There was no sign of life even about the windows. At last, I came to a kind of kitchen at the rear of the hall, where I found the mistress of the house and her servants, throng at their washing. When I had explained the purpose of my visit, the mistress pointed to a rude gate at the end, which opened to the front of the hall. I went through and found myself in a little green paddock, where there was not even one rose left "to mark where a garden had been." There were the principal windows,—one little window looking out from George Fox's study; the other two were old-fashioned bay windows, much larger. Between these was the small old doorway, to which two rude stone steps led up. All else was plain and unpretending; and all other windows in the lower part of the frontage were built up. Inside, I was shown the "hall," a quaint, flagged apartment, on the ground floor, with a great old-fashioned fire-place, and a kind of stone dais in the recess of the mullioned window. Here, I was told, the earliest meetings of the "Friends" were held. From this room, two steps led up to the little solemn sanctuary which was Fox's study; and I felt as if every footfall there was an intrusion; for that dim-lighted room, with its tiny lattice and quaint furniture, was the cell of a saint, "of whom the world was not worthy." His bed has been removed from its ancient apartment into a room where the farm servants sleep; and I was told that his Bible is now in the possession of a lady belonging to the Society of Friends, in Ulverstone. Before Fox married the pious widow of Judge Fell, he was once dragged from this house and imprisoned all night in Ulverstone, under a guard of fifteen men, some of whom were perched in the fireplace, for fear that he should fly up the chimney, and so escape. From thence he was removed to Lancaster Castle, where he suffered a long imprisonment. George Fox seems to have turned Ulverstone and the country about it upside down in those days, preaching in all sorts of pulpits and private houses, and sometimes in the open market-place. He was once shamefully maltreated in the churchyard of St Mary's, at Ulverstone, after preaching to the congregation there. About a quarter of a mile west of the hall there is a plain substantial chapel,—the first chapel of the disciples of George Fox,—built at his own cost, in 1688. It stands in a little flagged

GEORGE FOX'S CHAPEL, ON SWARTHMOOR.

enclosure, surrounded by a stone wall about nine feet high. The white door of the yard was open when I saw it, and the "Friends" were met within,—yet there was no sound, but the sea breeze whistling across the fields of Swarthmoor. Above the entrance was this inscription, plainly graven, "Ex dono, G. F., 1688." At the western end of the chapel there is a croft, which was presented with the chapel, for the accommodation of the horses of such Friends as came from a distance.

About a mile west of Fox's Chapel, a byeway leads into the old Roman road, at a place where a tesselated pavement was found a few years ago. A mile further in the same direction brings us to the bleak summit of "Birkrigg," which commands a new and extensive prospect of the bay, and its north and eastern shores. The pretty village of Bardsea is full in sight, at the foot of the hill. On the southern slope of this rocky moorland there is a small Druidical temple,—a circle of nine hoary stones, which, with one exception, are still more or less upright. A quarter of a mile west of this relic of British history, and near an antique farmhouse, called "Sunbreak," there is a lonely burial ground, looking out towards the sea. This is the oldest graveyard of the Society of Friends. It is surrounded by a high stone wall, and carefully kept in order. The door is generally locked, but I found it simply fastened with a staple and chain, and a wooden peg. The interior contains no visible commemoration of the dead; but a thick swathe of the greenest grass covers the whole area, save on the higher side, where picturesque fragments of limestone rock, rising above the rich herbage, are so beautifully bemossed here and there, that it seems as if nature, in her quiet, lovely way, had taken in hand to keep the memories of these nameless tenants of the dust for ever green. There was something more touchingly beautiful, more suggestive of repose, in the recordless silence of this lone graveyard of the persecuted puritan, than in any cemeteries adorned with grand efforts of monumental art—which so oft intrude upon the solemnity of death things sullied by the vanities of the living. The sacred simplicity of the spot made one feel more deeply how sound they slept below, in that unassailable shelter from the hurtful world. The very seabreeze seemed to pause there, and pass over this place of unawaking dreamers in a kind of requiem-hush.

Gleaston Castle is about six miles from Ulverstone. The direct road to it lies through the old village of Urswick. At the end of this village there is a fine tarn close by the highway. The people of Urswick Vale have a legend that the ruins of an ancient town lie beneath the waters of this tarn. Near Urswick there is the small monastic ruin of Bolton Chapel, standing in a farm-yard, by the road, and now used as a cowhouse. Leaving this village, we pass Redmond Hall, the seat of a family once known in English history. About a mile from Gleaston Castle, in a hollow of the fields, on the left hand side of the road, there is a pretty little sheet of water, called Mere Tarn, swarming with pike. The ruins of Gleaston Castle are of con-

GLEASTON CASTLE.

siderable extent. The castle originally consisted of four square towers, connected by strong curtain walls, defending an enclosure, the length of which seemed to me about one hundred yards. One of these towers has disappeared, and the other three are more or less ruinous; but the summits of two may yet be easily ascended by the stone steps which wind up in the thickness of the massive walls. In its palmy days, this castle must have looked imposing in the heart of the little vale, where it seems to have been placed more for shelter and seclusion than for anything commanding in position. It was built by the Flemings, lords of the ancient manor of Much Land. The possessions of Michael le Fleming were the only lands in all Furness exempted from the grant made by Stephen, Earl of Bologne and Moreton, to Furness Abbey. The name of this Michael, which the natives pronounce "Mickle," still clings to old associations in this neighbourhood, as in the case of "Mickle Well," not meaning great well, but "Michael's Well." I remember how, on that breezy day, when, with two friends, I visited the ruins of this castle, as we were casting about Gleaston in hungry search of a dinner, we found this old well in a mossy corner at the entrance of the village. The stones about it were worn by the footing of many generations, and the water was so clear that I could have seen a single thread of a lady's hair at the bottom of it. I remember, too, that when we were beginning to despair of finding anything like substantial refreshment, we met with it at the very last house on the western edge of the village, a clean little hostelry, where we got an excellent dinner of eggs and bacon, cheese, ale, pickles, salad fresh from the garden behind the house, and three quarts of buttermilk; in addition to which, I had my shoe mended; and we were treated with more than common civility, all for the low charge of three and sixpence,—which was received with satisfaction. The way of the shoe business was this,—I had burst the seam of it, and it was getting squashy with wet, for we had had a delightfully rough tramp o'er moss and fell, and through miry bye-roads, that day. The good wife at the alehouse offered to get it mended for me whilst dinner was cooking. The old man lent me a shoe of his own to put on meanwhile. It was as hard as an iron pot; in fact, it had a considerable weight of iron work about it, and for any rough work, I felt that that one shoe was worth at least four pair such as mine. With one foot handicapped in this clog of iron and leather, I amused myself with walking about the clean floor of slate stone, listening to the difference of sound in my footsteps, which went "fuzz, clang—fuzz, clang," reminding me of the three bells of a little country church that I have heard of, one of which was sound, the next cracked, and the third mended with leather,—their united music amounting to a kind of "ding, dang, puff." The shoe came back mended before dinner was over, and a thrill of returning comfort went through my frame when I got it on, for I had felt as if walking with a wet dish-cloth round my foot a while before. As we returned through the village, one of my friends proposed that we should just look in upon a relation of his, an old shoemaker, and a quaint man, well versed in the folk lore of the district. He then led us up to one of the most comfortable-looking cottages I ever saw. The floor was as clean as a plate just laid down for dinner, the place smelt as sweet as an herb-stall, and all the polishable metal things shone like pools of water in moonlight. The cheerful old wife, whose ruddy face was bedded in a snowy old-fashioned cap, and whose eyes, in spite of age and spectacles looked as bright as the stars on a frosty night, rose from her arm-chair, and hobbled about with her crutch, smiling and talking, and talking and smiling, as if she didn't know exactly what to do to show that she was very fain. At last, opening the door of an inner room, where the hearty old fellow and his son sat at work, she said, "What, dinnet ye see wha's here?" Dropping his hammer, and brushing the dirt from his leather apron, the old man rose above six feet into the air, pushed up his spectacles, and shouted, "Why, it never is, sewer! It cannot be reightly, can it! It's nowt i'th warld else, aw declare! Well, this is a capper, hooivvir! What ye're reight good stuff for sore e'en, mon! Whatever quarter's th' wind in, at ye're blawn this gate on? Well, cum, cum; sit ye daan, an' let's mak use on ye while ye are here." "Ye hevn't hed ye're teea, aw warnd," said the good wife. But we were already primely filled with good things; and no other feast could have been so delightful as the genial welcome which the old couple gave us. The day, too, was waning, with an uncertain sky, and we had several miles to go. As we sat talking with the old man, a fine pair of new double-soled shooting boots stood at my elbow. I took them up, and asked what such a pair would cost. He said they couldn't be done like them under a pound. "But," said he, "ye sud ha' sin a shoe that I stitched abaat an haar sin, for some poor tramp. I nivver see a warse made shoe i' my life, I think. An' he couldn't hev hed 'em lang, nawther,—t' leather wur so fresh." As he went on talking, I slowly lifted my foot till it came fairly into his sight. "Hello!" said he, with a confused gaze, "What, wor it yaar shoe?" It was. "Well then," replied he, "All at I can say is, at yer wit's a deeal better nor yer understandin'!" We had a good deal of gleeful talk with the old folk; after which six miles' walk in a high wind through the vale of Urswick brought us to Ulverstone, at the edge of dark, well pleased with our day's ramble.

Conishead Priory is rather more than a mile south of Ulverstone. There is a good road through the finest part of Conishead Park to the pretty village of Bardsea, which village is about three miles from Ulverstone. The road goes near the princely mansion, the seat of the Braddylls, which stands upon the site of the ancient priory. The entrance hall retains some relics of the old monastic buildings. About a mile beyond the priory, Bardsea Hall stands at the right hand side of the road, in a sheltered spot under the woods, and almost hidden from the traveller by a high wall. This quaint building was erected by the Molyneux family, as a hunting seat, and it is supposed to occupy the site of the ancient hospital of Bardsea, the oldest ecclesiastical

CONISHEAD PRIOYR.

establishment in Furness. This religious house was in existence in the latter part of the eleventh century, and had disappeared before the foundation of Conishead Priory. The best view of the Priory, and its beautiful park scenery, is from the summit of the woods behind Bardsea Hall.

Bardsea takes its name from the British word, "Bertesig," a place of thickets, as it appears in Doomsday Book. The village is pleasantly situated on a green eminence sloping gently to the sands. The woods, and dells, and quiet shore of this pretty sea-side nook, are full of pleasant walks. There is an antique mansion called "The Well House," which is an object of interest. In the village there are two respectable inns, and I found comfortable fare at the Cavendish Arms, where the landlord, Mr. Gilchrist, a gallant, old, retired preventive officer, from Cumberland, delighted me with his tales of wild adventure among the smugglers on the Scottish border, in "auld lang syne."

Aldingham is about three miles along the sea-side, west of Bardsea. The road goes through the extensive plantations of "Seawood," the property of the Crown; and through the old village of Baycliffe. The sea is either gleaming beautifully through the woods, or is in open sight, most of the way. Aldingham Church looks lonely standing there in its little grave-yard by the sea, as if musing on the old Saxon town long since devoured by the hungry waters. This was originally the parish church of the ancient manor of Much Land, which extended over the present Aldingham and Gleaston, and over several villages, such as Rhos, Lies, and Crimelton, which have been swallowed by the sea centuries ago. Nothing now remains of them but the account of their extent and value, preserved in the ancient records of Furness Abbey. This church is all that is left of the old town of Aldingham, the knightly residence and property of the Harringtons, one of which family, Lord de Harrington, died at the head of the Furness men, fighting for the Red Rose, at the battle of Wakefield. The church retains some parts of the original building in its round pillars, and in one of the doorways. The arms of the Harringtons appear in the east window. The rectory stands close to the church; and the present rector is the Rev. John Macaulay, brother of the famous historian and statesman.

Six miles by rail from Ulverstone, the magnificent ruins of Furness Abbey stand in the glen called "Bekanks Gill," or the Vale of the Deadly Nightshade, a sylvan seclusion, so cloistral in its character, that it might have been intended by nature to receive the grand pile, whose "bare ruined choirs" now lend such an impressive charm to the scene. This famous abbey was endowed with extraordinary wealth and power; and its prelates were temporal princes, ruling with almost absolute sway over a district as large as the Isle of Man; and yet, those white-robed monks from Savigny, and their successors, were the humanising mediators between feudal tyranny and serfdom, in the rough old days. I am told that the language of

T. H. WILSON, DEL.

FURNESS ABBEY,

the common people of Furness still retains French words and idioms not found elsewhere in Lancashire,—lingering relics of the secular influence of the foreign ecclesiastics who ruled this remote corner of England so long. It would be easy to give an architectural description of the ruins from careful works already written, but I refrain partly from want of room, and partly because the visitor can buy all that information for a trifle on the spot itself. I may say, however, that in addition to the general effect, the high altar with its beautiful sedilia, the chapter-house, and the Abbot's private chapel,

CHAPTER HOUSE, FURNESS ABBEY.

were particularly interesting to me. Though this monastery has lost the grand proportions of its old completeness, it is still robed in beauty, that "sole permanence in being's ceaseless flow;" and kind nature is quietly claiming its remains for her own again. It is a spot to linger in until the solemn beauty of it becomes an enduring treasure of the spirit. Reading the ancient charter of its foundation, I was so struck with the beauty of one passage in it, that I think the reader will excuse me for repeating it here. The words are as follows, from "West's Antiquities of Furness":—"In the name of the Blessed Trinity, and in honour of St. Mary of Furness, I, Stephen, Earl of Bologne and Moreton, consulting God, and providing for the safety of my own soul, the soul of my wife the Countess Matilda, the soul of my lord and uncle Henry King of England and Duke of Normandy, and for the souls of all the faithful, living as well as dead; in the year of our Lord 1127 of the Roman indiction, and the 5th and 18th of the Epact; considering every day the uncertainty of life, that the roses and flowers of kings, emperors, and dukes, and the crowns and palms of all the great, wither and decay; and that all things, with an uninterrupted course, tend to dissolution and death: I therefore return, give, and grant to God and St. Mary of Furness, all Furness and Walney," &c., &c.

Dalton, the ancient capital of Furness, is about a mile from the abbey, and four from Ulverstone. The Roman road from Maryport to Lancaster passes through this town, and it was the site of a Roman station (Galacum). In Saxon times, this town belonged to Earl Tosti. Later, it was the manor court and market town of the abbots of Furness, the square tower of whose castle now stands looking with an antique frown upon the market-place. Here the civil business of their vast possessions was transacted. The

DALTON CASTLE.

courts baron of Dalton are still held in this tower. Dalton church stands hard by the castle, near the edge of a steep rock, overlooking the vale of Deadly Nightshade. Romney, the painter, who was a native of this parish, lies buried in this graveyard, under a plain stone, bearing the name, dates, and the words, "Pictor celeberrimus." The parish of Dalton was almost depopulated by the great plague, two centuries ago. In the church there is a massive old stone font, carved with the armorial bearings of the ancient feudal lords of the district. This venerable relic stood for some time in the church-yard, exposed to mutilation and wear of the elements, until, through the good taste of the Rev. Mr. Morgan, the present vicar, it was removed to the interior again.

Peel Castle is about nine miles from Ulverstone, by rail, passing Furness Abbey, to Peel pier. A boat may be had at the pier, to the island, which is immediately opposite, divided from the main land by a narrow channel. Going by way of Barrow the distance by rail is about twelve miles; but the route is more varied. No other way of approaching the ruins of this fortress

PEEL CASTLE.

is so impressive as by a boat from Barrow, which is easily obtained, especially if "civil old Joe Winder" be about. This route also gives the tourist a good opportunity of seeing the harbour, in which the British navy might ride safely in the wildest weather. The isle of Walney, Rampside, and the most characteristic objects of this remote nook of the Furness shore, are in sight from the water. Barrow itself is an interesting spot. It is now the great port of Furness, and a place of increasing importance. Here, most of the ore of the district is shipped for Carron and Swansea, where it is used to enrich the poorer ores of Scotland and Wales. Hollinshed says that the Scots, in the reign of Edward the Second, during one of their raids into England, "met with no iron worth their notice until they came to Furness, in Lancashire, where they seized all the manufactured iron they could find, and carried it off with the greatest joy, though so heavy of carriage, and preferred it to all other plunder." In Barrow and its neighbourhood, as in many other parts of Furness, roads, houses, cattle, and men are more or less coloured with oxide of iron. A Furness miner, when disguised in his Sunday clothes, is seldom slow to tell you that he has "taen his degrees i' th' Red Lone College." The view of Peel Castle, as the boat nears the island from Barrow, is very striking. The castle was built by the Abbots of Furness, in the reign of Edward the Third, upon an older foundation, supposed to be the remains of a Danish fortress. These fierce sea-rovers often ravaged this part of the coast, and the terrors of their name linger yet among its traditions. The castle has been a place of much greater extent and strength than now appears. On the eastern side of the island, where high tides wash the base of the ruins, immense blocks of wall, which have been many years among the waters, are yet as firmly held together by their old cement as if they were solid rock. On the east and southern sides, the sea now covers a great extent of the old foundations, which are visible, here and there, under water. On the north and western sides, the two great ditches, the double lines of wall, and the strong flanking towers, still give some idea of the strength of the ancient defences. Near the ruins, there are two cottages, where the only inhabitants of the island reside. The largest of these cottages is a public-house, chiefly frequented by sailors from the harbours. Here the visitor may get good plain fare.

Coniston Lake is about an hour's ride, by rail from Ulverstone, on the Furness and Ulverstone line. The line goes by Kirby, the village of Broughton, on the Duddon shore, Woodlands, and Torver; and then along the western bank of the lake, with the "Old Man" and other Coniston mountains rising up from the left hand side of the line. The station is at Coniston village, near the head of the lake. This line runs a considerable distance by Duddon Sands, commanding an extensive view of the estuary.

Newby Bridge, at the foot of Windermere, is nine miles from Ulverstone. A coach starts thither from the latter place every day in summer. The road is full of interesting variety, winding by the banks of the river Leven almost all the way. On the right hand the upper part of the estuary stretches out from near the highway, bounded by the fells and beautiful shores of Cartmel; on the left, the green hills of Low Furness throw their shadows, here and there, across the way. The river Leven brings down the waters of Windermere to the sea. About four miles on the road, the beautiful valley of the Crake opens up on the western side, and the summits of the Coniston range are in sight. Through this valley the river Crake empties the waters of Coniston into the Leven. If any sojourner at Ulverston desires a fine walk through picturesque scenery, let him go about two miles along this high road from Ulverstone, then up Newland Vale about a mile, and then northward across the hills

CONISTON LAKE AND OLD MAN.

GREENODD.

a mile and a half, down to the village of Penny Bridge, at which spot he may be safely left to the influence of the scene. From these high grounds, between Newland Vale and Crake Vale, there are glorious views of the Coniston mountains. Near the entrance of the Crake valley the road passes the picturesque little village and port of Greenodd, in a nook of the estuary. A short distance from Greenodd, over the hills, there is an interesting old Baptist chapel, built in the intolerant days of the "Five Mile Act." At Backbarrow —where a stranger may be surprised to find a cotton-mill in such a spot— the river Leven falls over the rocks beautifully on the right-hand side of the road. Thence, to Newby Bridge, the road lies through a delightful woodland scene between the hills, with the river shining and singing all the way over its old bed of mossy rocks, down in the left-hand hollow. The old mansion-like inn, called the White Swan, is delightfully situated by the clear Leven side. In front, a quaint bridge of five arches spans the stream, and a few yards below it the river runs over a little fall, filling the quiet vale with its drowsy song by night and day. Above the bridge, the water comes down from Windermere through lovely scenery, gradually narrowing from a lake to a river, with the current of water scarcely discernible. The picturesque old inn, the bridge, the river, the drowsy fall, the choral woods, and every object in the hollow of this green nest of the mountains, is full of beauty and repose; and the hills that shut them in from the rest of the world heighten the general charm. The clear river glides by the front of the inn, with only the road between. It is pleasant to sit at the upper windows, or on the green flower-garnished benches below, in a still summer evening, listening to the birds and the waterfall, and watching the fish leaping up from the glittering water, as if giving a last frolicsome defiance to the cooks at the White Swan. At Newby Bridge we are on the very doorstep of that beautiful region of England—the Lake Country, and—

> "All that creation's varying mass assumes
> Of grand or lovely, here aspires and blooms;
> Bold rise the mountains, rich the gardens glow,
> Bright lakes expand, and conquering rivers flow."

Perhaps the finest views to be had in the immediate neighbourhood of Newby Bridge are from the summit of Finsthwaite, a lofty wooded height which rises steeply from the western side of the inn. On the top there is a square tower of slate stone, commemorative of the naval victories of England. The inside walls are written all over with names and nameless reliques. The key of the tower may be had at the White Swan. A footpath leads through the plantations to the summit, which is a singular mixture of craggy wildness and pretty woodland walks. Finsthwaite commands a glorious extent and variety of scenery in this land of lake and mountain. Southward, the vale of the Leven winds away to Ulverstone Sands; westward, the mountains of Coniston; eastward, the fells and vales of Cartmel; and northward, from

BACKBARROW MILLS.

WINDERMERE.

the foot of the hill, the entire length of crystal Windermere, dotted with its emerald isles, is in full view. Beyond, the most kingly cluster of all our English mountains bounds the landscape. Green is "the favourite colour of God," and the green shores of this garden-girt water are of a brightness such as is rarely met with elsewhere in the world. Looking upon Windermere from Finsthwaite, on a sunny day, one may say in the words of Tom Moore, that Nature seems to have lavished her charms upon the scene—

> "To make a heaven for love to sigh in,
> For bards to live and saints to die in."

The distance from Newby Bridge to Kendal, by way of Cartmel Fells, is ten miles; by Leven Bridge, fifteen miles. An omnibus goes from the inn twice a day in summer through Cartmel to the village of Grange. Steamers start daily in summer to Ambleside and back, calling at Bowness. There are ample facilities for boating and fishing; and, in addition to this, I believe there is hardly a house of entertainment in the lake country more notable for genuine comfort and the general excellence of its accommodation, than the White Swan at Newby Bridge.

A. IRELAND AND CO., PRINTERS, PALL MALL, MARKET STREET, MANCHESTER.

OVER SANDS TO THE LAKES;

BY

EDWIN WAUGH,

AUTHOR OF "SKETCHES OF LANCASHIRE LIFE AND LOCALITIES," "COME WHOAM TO THI CHILDER AN' ME," ETC., ETC.

A. IRELAND & CO., 22, MARKET STREET, MANCHESTER;

AND ALL BOOKSELLERS AND NEWS VENDORS.

1860.

CPSIA information can be obtained
at www.ICGtesting.com
Printed in the USA
BVOW06s2049010517
482841BV00014B/230/P

9 781332 232710